PRE-APPRENTICESHIP
MATHS & LITERACY FOR
PLUMBING

graduated exercises and practice exam

Andrew Spencer

 **A+ National**

NELSON
A Cengage Company

A+ National Pre-apprenticeship Maths & Literacy for Plumbing
1st Edition
Andrew Spencer

Associate publishing editor: Jana Raus
Project editor: Jana Raus
Senior designer: Vonda Pestana
Text design: Vonda Pestana
Cover design: Ami-Louise Sharpe
Cover image: Shutterstock/Lisa F. Young
Photo researcher: Libby Henry
Production controller: Alex Ross
Reprint: Katie McCappin
Typeset by Macmillan Publishing Services

Any URLs contained in this publication were checked for currency during the production process. Note, however, that the publisher cannot vouch for the ongoing currency of URLs.

Acknowledgements
We would like to thank the following for permission to reproduce copyright material:

Jupiterimages Corporation: p. 21; Photolibrary: pp. 18, 29.

Every effort has been made to trace and acknowledge copyright. However, if any infringement has occurred the publishers tender their apologies and invite the copyright holders to contact them.

For product information and technology assistance,
in Australia call **1300 790 853**;
in New Zealand call **0800 449 725**

For permission to use material from this text or product, please email **aust.permissions@cengage.com**

ISBN 978 0 17 047337 8

Cengage Learning Australia
Level 7, 80 Dorcas Street
South Melbourne, Victoria Australia 3205

Cengage Learning New Zealand
Unit 4B Rosedale Office Park
331 Rosedale Road, Albany, North Shore 0632, NZ

For learning solutions, visit **cengage.com.au**

Printed in Australia by Ligare Pty Limited.
1 2 3 4 5 6 7 26 25 24 23 22

A+ National
PRE-APPRENTICESHIP
Maths & Literacy for Plumbing

Contents

Introduction

It has always been important to understand, from a teacher's perspective, the nature of the mathematical skills students need for their future, rather than teaching them textbook mathematics. This has been a guiding principle behind the development of the content in this workbook. To teach maths that is *relevant* to students seeking apprenticeships is the best that we can do, to give students an education in the field that they would like to work in.

The content in this resource is aimed at the level that is needed for a student to have the best possibility of improving their maths and literacy skills specifically for trades. Students can use this workbook to prepare for an apprenticeship entry assessment, or even to assist with basic numeracy and literacy at the VET/TAFE level. Coupled with the NelsonNet website, https://www.nelsonnet.com.au/free-resources, these resources have the potential to improve the students' understanding of basic maths concepts that can be applied to trades. These resources have been trialled, and they work.

Commonly used trade terms are introduced so that students have a basic understanding of terminology that they will encounter in the workplace environment. Students who can complete this workbook and reach an 80 per cent or higher outcome in all topics will have achieved the goal of this resource. These students will go on to complete work experience, do a VET accredited course or be able to gain entry into VET/TAFE or an apprenticeship in the trade of their choice.

The content in this workbook is the first step towards bridging the gap between what has been learnt in previous years, and what needs to be remembered and re-learnt for use in trades. Students will significantly benefit from the consolidation of the basic maths and literacy concepts.

Every school has students who want to work with their hands, and not all students want to go to university. The best students want to learn what they do not know; and if students want to learn, this book has the potential to give them a good start in life.

This resource has been specifically tailored to prepare students for sitting apprenticeship or VET/TAFE admission tests, and for giving students the basic skills they will need for a career in trade. In many ways, it is a win–win situation, with students enjoying and studying relevant maths for trades and Registered Training Organisations (RTOs) receiving students that have improved basic maths and literacy skills.

All that is needed is patience, hard work, a positive attitude, a belief in yourself that you can do it and a desire to achieve. The rest is up to you.

About the author

Andrew Spencer has studied education within both Australia and overseas. He has a Bachelor of Education, as well as a Masters of Science in which he specialised in teacher education. Andrew has extensive experience in teaching secondary mathematics throughout New South Wales and South Australia for well over fifteen years. He has taught a range of subject areas, including Maths, English, Science, Classics, Physical Education and Technical Studies. His sense of the importance of practical mathematics has continued to develop with the range of subject areas he has taught in.

Acknowledgements

For Paula, Zach, Katelyn, Mum and Dad.

Many thanks to Mal Aubrey (GTA) and all training organisations for their input.

Thanks also to the De La Salle Brothers for their selfless support and ongoing work with all students.

To Dr Pauline Carter for her unwavering support of all Maths teachers.

This is for all students who value learning, who are willing to work hard and who have character . . . and are characters!

Unit 1: Spelling

Short-answer questions

Specific instructions to students

- This exercise will help you to identify and correct spelling errors.
- Read the following question and then answer accordingly.

Read the following passage and identify and correct the spelling errors.

A plumber needs to re-fit a bathroom. It needs a signifikant amount of work. The toilet needs a new cisctern, as well as a new bowl. In addision, the sinc and the shouwer need to be replased. The cost of the new parts is a magor considerution. The managor wants the job completed by Saturduy. The aprentice replaces most of the parts on the toliet first, and then moves on to secure the base currectly.

There are a numbar of rings that need replacing, along with several wushers. The showur skreen has a damiged hunge that will need to be removed and repared. The apprentise uses a skrewdriver to remove the six screws on the hinge. One is dufficult to remove, so he sprays the screw with lubricant and then uses a different screwdrivur to remove it. The boss indikates that the he waunts the watur turned off before proceding. The old toilet bowl has suveral deep skratches in it and it therefor needs to be thrown out. It takes ovur eight hours to complete the job; however, everything turns out well and is finished by the time to pack up comes aroond.

Incorrect words:

_____

_____

_____

Correct words:

_____

_____

_____

Unit 2: Alphabetising

Put the following words into alphabetical order.

Conduit	Copper tubing
Cistern	Pipe length
Shower	PVC
Porcelain	Threaded pipe
Pipe	Angles
Sealant	Flange
Gloves	

_____

_____

_____

_____

_____

_____

_____

_____

_____

_____

_____

_____

Short-answer questions

Specific instructions to students

- This is an exercise to help you understand what you read.
- Read the following passage and then answer the questions that follow.

Read the following passage and answer the questions in sentence form.

Paul the Plumber had to be onsite early on Monday to work on a sewer pipe that had burst. He arrived at 6.45 a.m. and he first surveyed the site where most of the leakage had occurred. One of his crew had to go to hospital the previous day as he had injured his shoulder lifting a heavy pipe into place. He was going to be off sick that day and Paul had several other plumbers to supervise. When the apprentice, Geoff, arrived Paul immediately met with him to ensure he would have jobs to complete. A number of copper pipes needed replacing and Geoff was the man for the job. While Paul set Geoff up for the work, the other plumber, Andrew, arrived. He was allocated the task of the major leakage fault, which Paul would also be working on. They found that the pipe had been ruptured by a bobcat that had been at the site the day before. There was extensive damage and they needed to make sure that the water was turned off. However, before Paul or Andrew could begin the job, their first priority was to make sure that the area was safe to work in.

Andrew returned to the work vehicle to get some tools while Paul made everything ready. Meanwhile, Geoff was busy measuring the lengths of copper pipes that needed replacing. He inspected the pipes and measured each of the lengths. The job was not difficult, but he knew that at some stage he would need to weld the pipes. He went to the work vehicle, got out the welder and started setting it up. He asked Paul's advice about the best way to weld the pipes and so Paul came over to give Geoff a hand. Within two hours they had completed the job, leaving both Geoff and Paul free to assist Andrew in fixing the major leakage. It was in the middle of winter, and so both the sun and the afternoon quickly drew to a close. The crew finished up at 4.30 p.m., knowing that they would need to return early next morning to complete their work.

QUESTION 1

Why did Paul have to be onsite early?

Answer:

QUESTION 2

What was the first job that Paul needed to do?

Answer:

QUESTION 3

Who replaced the copper pipes?

Answer:

QUESTION 4

Why did Geoff ask Paul for advice?

Answer:

QUESTION 5

How long was Paul's working day? State your answer in hours and minutes.

Answer:

9780170473378

MATHEMATICS

Unit 4: General Mathematics

Short-answer questions

Specific instructions to students

- This unit will help you to improve your general mathematical skills.
- Read the questions below and answer all of them in the spaces provided.
- No calculators.
- You will need to show all working.

QUESTION 1

What unit of measurement would you use to measure:

a length of copper pipe?

Answer:

_____

the temperature of water?

Answer:

_____

the amount of drain cleaner in a bottle?

Answer:

_____

the weight of a toilet?

Answer:

_____

the flow rate of water?

Answer:

_____

the amount of pipe sealant?

Answer:

_____

the cost of a piece of pipe?

Answer:

_____

QUESTION 2

Write an example of the following and give an example of where it may be found in the plumbing industry.

a percentages

Answer:

_____

b decimals

Answer:

_____

c fractions

Answer:

_____

d mixed numbers

Answer:

_____

e ratios

Answer:

_____

_____

f angles

Answer:

_____

QUESTION 3
Convert the following units.

a 12 kg to grams

Answer:

_____

b 4 t to kilograms

Answer:

_____

c 120 cm to metres

Answer:

_____

d 1140 mL to litres

Answer:

_____

e 1650 g to kilograms

Answer:

_____

f 1880 kg to tonnes

Answer:

_____

g 13 m to centimetres

Answer:

_____

h 4.5 L to millilitres

Answer:

_____

QUESTION 4
Write the following in descending order:

0.4   0.04   4.1   40.0   400.00   4.0

Answer:

_____

QUESTION 5
Write the decimal number that is between:

a 0.2 and 0.4

Answer:

_____

b 1.8 and 1.9

Answer:

_____

c 12.4 and 12.6

Answer:

_____

d 28.3 and 28.4

Answer:

_____

e 101.5 and 101.7

Answer:

_____

QUESTION 6
Round off the following numbers to two (2) decimal places.

a 12.346

Answer:

_____

b 2.251

Answer:

_____

c 123.897

Answer:

_____

 9780170473378

d 688.882

Answer:

_____

e 1209.741

Answer:

_____

QUESTION 7
Estimate the following by approximation.

a 1288 × 19 =

Answer:

_____

b 201 × 20 =

Answer:

_____

c 497 × 12.2 =

Answer:

_____

d 1008 × 10.3 =

Answer:

_____

e 399 × 22 =

Answer:

_____

f 201 − 19 =

Answer:

_____

g 502 − 61 =

Answer:

_____

h 1003 − 49 =

Answer:

_____

i 10 001 − 199 =

Answer:

_____

j 99.99 − 39.8 =

Answer:

_____

QUESTION 8
What do the following add up to?

a $4, $4.99 and $144.95

Answer:

_____

b 8.75, 6.9 and 12.55

Answer:

_____

c 65 mL, 18 mL and 209 mL

Answer:

_____

d 21.3 g, 119 g and 884.65 g

Answer:

_____

QUESTION 9
Subtract the following.

a 2338 from 7117

Answer:

_____

b 1786 from 3112

Answer:

_____

c 5979 from 8014

Answer:

_____

d 11 989 from 26 221

Answer:

_____

e 108 767 from 231 111

Answer:

_____

QUESTION 10

Use division to solve the following:

a 2177 ÷ 7 =

Answer:

_____

b 4484 ÷ 4 =

Answer:

_____

c 63.9 ÷ 0.3 =

Answer:

_____

d 121.63 ÷ 1.2 =

Answer:

_____

e 466.88 ÷ 0.8 =

Answer:

_____

The following information is provided for Question 11.

_____

To solve using BODMAS, in order from left to right, solve the Brackets first, then Of, then Division, then Multiplication, then Addition and lastly Subtraction. The following example has been done for your reference.

EXAMPLE

Solve $(4 \times 7) \times 2 + 6 - 4$.

STEP 1

Solve the Brackets first: $(4 \times 7) = 28$

STEP 2

No Division, so next solve Multiplication: $28 \times 2 = 56$

STEP 3

Addition is next: $56 + 6 = 62$

STEP 4

Subtraction is the last process: $62 - 4 = 58$

FINAL ANSWER

58
_____

QUESTION 11

Using BODMAS, solve:

a $(6 \times 9) \times 5 + 7 - 2 =$

Answer:

_____

b $(9 \times 8) \times 4 + 6 - 1 =$

Answer:

_____

c $3 \times (5 \times 7) + 11 - 8 =$

Answer:

_____

d $5 \times (8 \times 3) + 9 - 6 =$

Answer:

_____

e $7 + 6 \times 3 + (9 \times 6) - 9 =$

Answer:

_____

f $6 + 9 \times 4 + (6 \times 7) - 21 =$

Answer:

_____

Section A: Addition

QUESTION 1

To put down pipe for a drain, a plumber uses 2 m, 1 m, 3 m and 5 m and 7 m of pipe. How much pipe has he used in total?

Answer:

QUESTION 2

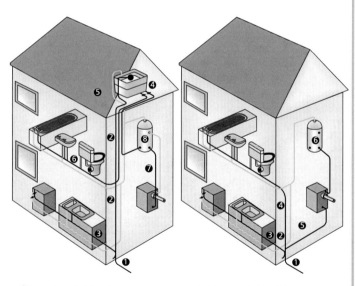

Indirect water system
1 service pipe from water company
2 rising main
3 drinking water from rising main
4 cold-water storage tank
5 overflow pipe
6 cold feed pipe to bathroom
7 cold feed pipe to boiler
8 hot-water cylinder

Direct water system
1 service pipe from water company
2 rising main
3 drinking water to kitchen
4 drinking water to bathroom
5 cold feed pipe to boiler
6 hot-water cylinder

To re-plumb a bathroom, toilet and shower, a plumber uses 2.5 m, 1.8 m, 3.3 m and 5.2 m of pipe. How much pipe has been used in total?

Answer:

QUESTION 3

A plumber stocks 127 washing machine water hoses, 368 hoses that are 25 mm in diameter and 723 various other hoses. How many hoses, in total, are in stock?

Answer:

QUESTION 4

A plumber drives 352 km, 459 km, 4872 km and 198 km. How far has the car been driven in total?

Answer:

QUESTION 5

An apprentice plumber uses the following amounts of diesel over a month:

Week 1: 35.5 L

Week 2: 42.9 L

Week 3: 86.9 L

Week 4: 66.2 L

a How many litres have been used in total?

Answer:

_____

b If diesel costs $1.95 per litre, how much would fuel have cost for the month?

Answer:

_____

QUESTION 6

If an apprentice buys a tap fitting for $12.50, 4 plungers for $16.80 and a hose for $6.75, how much has been spent all together?

Answer:

_____

QUESTION 7

The following are used to complete three jobs: 26 nuts on one job, 52 nuts on the second job and 48 nuts on the third job. How many nuts have been used?

Answer:

_____

QUESTION 8

Some plastic fittings are bought for $125.80, a toilet for $166.99 and a new tap fitting for $88.50. How much has been spent?

Answer:

_____

QUESTION 9

An apprentice travels 36.8 km, 98.7 km, 77.2 km and 104.3 km over four days. How far has the apprentice travelled in total?

Answer:

_____

QUESTION 10

To complete some plumbing work on a home, 178 bolts, 188 nuts and 93 washers are used. How many parts are used?

Answer:

_____

Section B: Subtraction

Short-answer questions

Specific instructions to students

- This section will help you to improve your subtraction skills for basic operations.
- Read the following questions and answer all of them in the spaces provided.
- No calculators.
- You will need to show all working.

QUESTION 1

A vehicle is filled with petrol to its limit of 52 L. If the driver uses 22 L on one trip, 17 L on the second trip and 11 L on the third trip, how much is left in the tank?

Answer:

_____

QUESTION 2

If one plumber travels 362 km and another plumber travels 169 km, how much farther has the first plumber gone than the second?

Answer:

_____

9780170473378

QUESTION 3

P-plate driver A uses 243.8 L of LPG in one month and P-plate driver B uses 147.9 L of LPG in the same month. How much more LPG does P-plate driver A use?

Answer:

_____

QUESTION 4

An apprentice uses 39 nuts from a box that has contained 200 nuts. How many nuts are now left?

Answer:

_____

QUESTION 5

A service on a car costs $224.65. The mechanic takes off a discount of 10%, which is then rounded off to $25.00. How much does the customer need to pay after the discount?

Answer:

_____

QUESTION 6

Over a year, an apprentice drives 12 316 km. Of this, 5787 km is for her own personal use. What distance did she travel for work purposes?

Answer:

_____

QUESTION 7

A plumber uses the following amounts of drain cleaner for three jobs:

Job 1: 5.5 L

Job 2: 3.8 L

Job 3: 6.9 L

How much drain cleaner is now left in a drum that originally contained 20 L of drain cleaner?

Answer:

_____

QUESTION 8

During one month, a plumber replaces 74 washers on several different jobs. If there were a total of 250 washers to begin with, how many are now left?

Answer:

_____

QUESTION 9

A plumber's work van has an odometer reading of 78 769 before the start of a year. At the end of the year it reads 84 231. What distance has the plumber travelled during the year?

Answer:

_____

QUESTION 10

A plumber uses the following amounts of the same 50 mm PVC pipe on three separate jobs: 8.7 m, 6.9 m and 15.3 m. If there were 50 m of pipe to begin with, how much is now left?

Answer:

_____

Section C: Multiplication

QUESTION 1

If a car travels at 60 km/h, how far will it travel in 4 hours?

Answer:

QUESTION 2

If a car travels at 80 km/h, how far will it travel in 7 hours?

Answer:

QUESTION 3

A plumber uses 15 L of fuel for one trip. How much fuel will he use if he needs to complete the same trip 26 more times?

Answer:

QUESTION 4

An apprentice plumber uses 12 nuts, 14 washers and 8 bolts to assemble one fixture. How many nuts, washers and bolts would be used on 144 more of the same fixture?

Answer:

QUESTION 5

To complete a job on a building, 5 m of pipe with a 75 mm diameter is used on one section of the building, 2 m of pipe with a 50 mm diameter is used on another section, and 8 m of pipe with a 25 mm diameter is used on the last section. How much of each pipe would be used for 19 similar jobs?

Answer:

QUESTION 6

To secure several bath fittings, a plumber uses 16 lock nuts. How many lock nuts would she need for 87 bath fittings?

Answer:

QUESTION 7

A work vehicle uses 9 L of LPG for every 100 km travelled. How much LPG would be used for 450 km?

Answer:

QUESTION 8

If a plumber used 73 spring washers on average per month, how many would he use over a year? (Note that there are 12 months in a year.)

Answer:

QUESTION 9

If a plumber uses 3 m of copper tubing each day over 28 days, how much tubing has she used in total?

Answer:

_____

QUESTION 10

If a car travels at 110 km/h for 5 hours, how far has it travelled?

Answer:

_____

Section D: Division

Short-answer questions

Specific instructions to students

- This section will help you to improve your division skills for basic operations.
- Read the following questions and answer all of them in the spaces provided.
- No calculators.
- You will need to show all working.

QUESTION 1

A plumber has a 24 m length of 25 mm PVC pipe. How many jobs can be completed if each standard job requires 3 m of pipe?

Answer:

_____

QUESTION 2

If a plumber earns $1125 (gross) for working a 5-day week, how much does the plumber earn per day?

Answer:

_____

QUESTION 3

A manager of a major plumbing company buys 14 000 L of fuel in bulk. Each of the fuel drums contains 180 L.

a How many drums are completely filled?

Answer:

_____

b Is any fuel left over?

Answer:

_____

QUESTION 4

An apprentice covers 78 km in a 5-day week. On average, how many kilometres per day has he travelled?

Answer:

_____

QUESTION 5

The total weight of a 4WD work vehicle is 1488 kg. How much load, in kilograms, is on each wheel?

Answer:

_____

QUESTION 6

A plumber covers 925 km over 27 days. How many kilometres has she covered, on average, each day?

Answer:

_____

QUESTION 7

During a yearly stocktake, a storeman at a plumbing company counts 648 washers. There are 110 washers in each box.

a How many boxes are there?

Answer:

_____

b Are any washers left over?

Answer:

_____

QUESTION 8

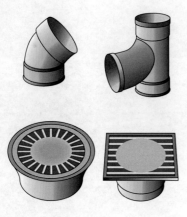

A plumber orders 40 m of PVC pipe with a 25 mm diameter. If it is cut into 8 m lengths, how many lengths are there in total?

Answer:

_____

QUESTION 9

A truck delivers 460 m of PVC pipe with a 50 mm diameter to a plumbing company. The piping will be used for 4 separate jobs, and the amount of piping for each job will be the same. How much piping will be allocated for each job?

Answer:

_____

QUESTION 10

A plumber travels over 890 km over 28 days. How many kilometres has he travelled, on average, each day?

Answer:

_____

9780170473378

Section A: Addition

QUESTION 1

A plumber buys a set of 4 tyres for a work vehicle, which comes to a total of $416.88. She then remembers that she needs a spare tyre, which costs another $45.50. What is the total cost of the 5 tyres?

Answer:

QUESTION 2

A plumber buys a circular saw for $39.95, a container of pipe glue for $29.95, several boxes of screws for a total of $44.55 and several hose clamps for $19.45. How much has been spent?

Answer:

QUESTION 3

Two lengths of 50 mm pipe measure 10.25 m and 8.48 m respectively. What is the total length?

Answer:

QUESTION 4

A plumber buys the following: a washing machine hose for $8.99, a spare belt for $6.50, lubricant for $12.30 and an air compressor for $65.90. What is the total cost?

Answer:

QUESTION 5

If an apprentice plumber travels 65.8 km, 36.5 km, 22.7 km and 89.9 km over a week, how far has he travelled in total?

Answer:

QUESTION 6

What is the total length of a screwdriver with a handle of 15.5 cm and an end of 7.8 cm?

Answer:

QUESTION 7

A pipe has a diameter of 54.2 mm. Another pipe has a diameter of 75.9 mm. What is the combined length of the diameters of both pipes?

Answer:

QUESTION 8

A plumber completes three jobs. The following bills are charged for each job: $450.80 for the first job, $1130.65 for the second job and $660.45 for the third job. How much has been charged in total for all 3 jobs?

Answer:

QUESTION 9

A length of copper pipe measures 7.5 m. Another length of the same pipe measures 9.8 m. What is the total length of both copper pipes?

Answer:

QUESTION 10

Four pipes each have different diameters: 50.5 mm, 75.5 mm, 50.8 mm and 75.3 mm. What is the total of the combined diameters?

Answer:

Section B: Subtraction

QUESTION 1

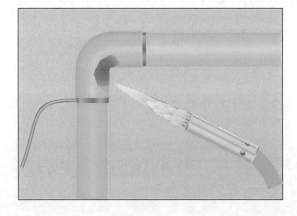

A length of 10 m copper pipe has several lengths cut from it. The lengths that were cut measured 3.8 m and 4.9 m respectively.

a How much has been cut off?

Answer:

b How much is left?

Answer:

QUESTION 2

If a 4 m length of 75 mm PVC pipe has 22.5 cm cut from it, what length now remains?

Answer:

QUESTION 3

A plumber completes a job that costs $789.20 and then gives a discount of $75.50. How much is the final cost of the job?

Answer:

QUESTION 4

An apprentice works 38 hours and earns $245.60. He spends $48.85 on food, petrol and union fees. How much does he take home?

Answer:

QUESTION 5

A connecting pipe is 65.60 cm in length. A length of 8.95 cm is cut off. What amount remains?

Answer:

_____

QUESTION 6

If one length of conduit has a diameter of 95.5 mm and another has a diameter of 88.5 mm, what is the difference between the two?

Answer:

_____

QUESTION 7

One pipe's diameter is 32.50 mm and another's is 12.85 mm. What is the difference?

Answer:

_____

QUESTION 8

A plumber uses a 4 L container of pipe glue for three different jobs: 285 mL for job 1, 560 mL for job 2, and 1300 mL on job 3. How much is left?

Answer:

_____

QUESTION 9

An apprentice has a 4 m length of 25 mm PVC pipe. If 35 cm is cut off, then 76 cm and a further 44 cm, how much is left?

Answer:

_____

QUESTION 10

A fitting needs to be reattached. If a plumber has a 6 m length of 50 mm PVC pipe and he then cuts 257 cm off, how much is left?

Answer:

_____

Section C: Multiplication

Short-answer questions

Specific instructions to students

- This section will help you to improve your multiplication skills when working with decimals.
- Read the following questions and answer all of them in the spaces provided.
- No calculators.
- You will need to show all working.

QUESTION 1

If a tap costs $19.95 and a plumber needs 5 taps, how much will the total cost be?

Answer:

_____

QUESTION 2

If a plumber uses 16 L of drain cleaner and 1 L costs $10.50, what is the total cost for 16 L?

Answer:

_____

QUESTION 3

The following plumbing components are replaced in a home: 6 washers at a cost of $0.50 each, and 8 spring washers at $0.99 each. What is the total cost?

Answer:

QUESTION 4

If a plumber uses 6 packets of nuts that cost $8.65 each, how much does he pay?

Answer:

QUESTION 5

An apprentice plumber purchases 12 packets of screws that cost $9.95 each from a hardware store. What is the total cost of the screws?

Answer:

QUESTION 6

An apprentice earns $13.50 per hour. If the apprentice works a 45-hour week, how much will she earn?

Answer:

QUESTION 7

A plumbing workshop owner buys laundry hose for $2.55 per metre. If 25 m are purchased, how much is the total cost?

Answer:

QUESTION 8

A plumber's work van has a 52 L tank. If petrol costs $1.55 per litre, how much would the total cost be for 52 L?

Answer:

QUESTION 9

A petrol station manager purchases 3400 L of petrol for $1.15 per litre. What is the outlay?

Answer:

QUESTION 10

A plumber earns $280.65 per day. If he works 5 days in one week, how much will he have earned?

Answer:

9780170473378

Section D: Division

Short-answer questions

Specific instructions to students

- This section will help you to improve your division skills when working with decimals.
- Read the following questions and answer all of them in the spaces provided.
- No calculators.
- You will need to show all working.

QUESTION 1

A plumber has 28.5 L of drain cleaner that is needed for 6 separate jobs. How much needs to be allocated for each job?

Answer:

QUESTION 2

A plumber earns $990.60 for 5 days of work. How much does she earn per day?

Answer:

QUESTION 3

The bill for work on a vanity unit comes to $302.70. If the plumber splits the total evenly between himself and his apprentice, how much does each get?

Answer:

QUESTION 4

A master plumber completes a job on a bathroom. If the cost of labour is $440.85 and it takes 8 hours to complete the job, how much is the hourly rate?

Answer:

QUESTION 5

A semitrailer delivering plumbing accessories drives from Adelaide to Darwin and covers 3568 km over 5 days. How far has been travelled, on average, each day?

Answer:

QUESTION 6

A contract plumber drives 889.95 km over 9 days. How far has he travelled each day?

Answer:

QUESTION 7

A car uses 72 L to travel 575.8 km. How far can the car travel per litre?

Answer:

QUESTION 8

A plumbing workshop buys 360 kitchen tap sets, in bulk, at a total cost of $12290. How much is the cost of one tap set?

Answer:

QUESTION 9

It costs $90.95 to fill a 52 L fuel tank. How much is the cost per litre?

Answer:

QUESTION 10

A 50 m roll of heater hose costs $83.60. How much does it cost per metre?

Answer:

Unit 7: Fractions

Section A: Addition

QUESTION 1

$\frac{1}{2} + \frac{4}{5} =$

Answer:

_____

QUESTION 2

$2\frac{2}{4} + 1\frac{2}{3} =$

Answer:

_____

QUESTION 3

A plumber pours $\frac{1}{3}$ of a bottle of pipe glue into a container. He then adds $\frac{1}{4}$ of another bottle into the same container. How much glue is in the container now in total? Express your answer as a fraction.

Answer:

_____

QUESTION 4

A bucket $\frac{1}{3}$ full of water is used to test some pipes. Another bucket is $\frac{1}{2}$ full. How much water is there in total? Express your answer as a fraction.

Answer:

_____

QUESTION 5

A plumber has $1\frac{2}{3}$ tubes of waterproof silicon. Another $1\frac{1}{4}$ tubes of the same silicon are also in the plumber's ute. How much waterproof silicon is there in total? Express your answer as a fraction.

Answer:

_____

Section B: Subtraction

QUESTION 1

$\frac{2}{3} - \frac{1}{4} =$

Answer:

_____

QUESTION 2

$2\frac{2}{3} - 1\frac{1}{4} =$

Answer:

_____

QUESTION 3

A plumber uses $\frac{2}{3}$ of a tube of sealant on a burst pipe. If a further $\frac{1}{2}$ of a tube is needed to complete the job, how much sealant is left in the tube? Express your answer as a fraction.

Answer:

_____

QUESTION 4

An apprentice has 3 bottles of drain cleaner. If $1\frac{2}{3}$ bottles of drain cleaner are used to clean a toilet, how much is left? Express your answer as a fraction.

Answer:

_____

QUESTION 5

A plumber has $2\frac{3}{4}$ tubes of silicon, and $1\frac{1}{2}$ tubes are used to seal an area in a shower. How much silicon is left in total? Express your answer as a fraction.

Answer:

_____

Section C: Multiplication

Short-answer questions

Specific instructions to students

- This section is designed to help you to improve your multiplication skills when working with fractions.
- Read the following questions and answer all of them in the spaces provided.
- No calculators.
- You will need to show all working.

QUESTION 1

$\frac{2}{4} \times \frac{2}{3} =$

Answer:

QUESTION 2

$2\frac{2}{3} \times 1\frac{1}{2} =$

Answer:

QUESTION 3

A plumber cuts 2 lengths of 75 mm downpipe, each measuring $18\frac{1}{2}$ cm. What is the total length cut? Work out the answer using fractions.

Answer:

QUESTION 4

A building needs $3\frac{1}{2}$ lengths of 50 mm conduit that each measure $15\frac{1}{2}$ cm. How much conduit is needed in total?

Answer:

QUESTION 5

A shower requires 4 lengths of $10\frac{1}{2}$ cm copper tubing to complete the job. How much copper tubing is needed in total? Work out the answer using fractions.

Answer:

Section D: Division

Short-answer questions

Specific instructions to students

- This section is designed to help you to improve your division skills when working with fractions.
- Read the following questions and answer all of them in the spaces provided.
- No calculators.
- You will need to show all working.

QUESTION 1

$\frac{2}{3} \div \frac{1}{4} =$

Answer:

_____

QUESTION 2

$2\frac{3}{4} \div 1\frac{1}{3} =$

Answer:

_____

QUESTION 3

An apprentice has a length of 25 mm pipe that measures $26\frac{1}{2}$ cm. The apprentice needs to cut $2\frac{1}{2}$ equal lengths of the pipe. How long is each piece?

Answer:

_____

QUESTION 4

An apprentice has $1\frac{2}{3}$ tubes of waterproof sealant. If the tubes are used on 3 separate jobs, how much will be used on each job? Express your answer as a fraction.

Answer:

_____

QUESTION 5

A plumber has $2\frac{2}{3}$ bottles of drain cleaner that are used on 2 jobs. How much is used on each job? Express your answer as a fraction.

Answer:

_____

Unit 8: Percentages

Short-answer questions

Specific instructions to students

- In this unit, you will be able to practise and improve your skills in working out percentages.
- Read the following questions and answer all of them in the spaces provided.
- No calculators.
- You will need to show all working.

> 10% rule: Move the decimal one place to the left to get 10%.

EXAMPLE

10% of $45.00 would be $4.50.

QUESTION 1

A repair bill for work on a kitchen unit, including parts and labour, comes to $220.00. How much is 10% of the bill?

Answer:

_____

QUESTION 2

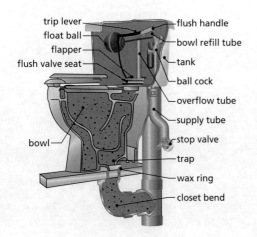

trip lever — flush handle
float ball — bowl refill tube
flapper — tank
flush valve seat — ball cock
— overflow tube
— supply tube
bowl — stop valve
— trap
— wax ring
— closet bend

A toilet costs $249.00.

a What is 10% of the cost?

Answer:

_____

b How much will the toilet cost when this discount is subtracted from the initial cost?

Answer:

_____

QUESTION 3

A workshop owner buys a 2 hp direct drive air compressor for $198.50. If he was given a 10% discount, how much would the air compressor cost? (Hint: Find 10% and subtract it from the cost of the air compressor.)

Answer:

_____

QUESTION 4

A plumber buys 5 L of sealant for $84.80. A 5% discount is then given. How much is paid? (Hint: Find 10%, halve it and then subtract it from $84.80.)

Answer:

_____

QUESTION 5

A trade assistant buys 3 roller storage bins for $20, a 12 V air compressor for $69 and a pipe bender for $169.

a How much is paid in total?

Answer:

_____

b How much is paid after a 10% discount?

Answer:

_____

QUESTION 6

The following items are purchased for a workshop: a fluorescent light for $39.99, a crimping toolkit for $9.99, a socket set for $39.99, a digital thermometer for $12.99, a set of screwdrivers for $49.99 and a 25 m extension lead for $14.99.

a How much is paid in total?

Answer:

_____

b What is the final cost after a 10% discount?

Answer:

_____

QUESTION 7

A plumbing store offers 20% off the cost of screwdriver sets. If a set is priced at $36 before the discount, how much will each set cost after the discount?

Answer:

_____

QUESTION 8

Wrenches are discounted by 15%. If the recommended retail price for a large wrench is $15.50 each, what is the discounted price?

Answer:

_____

QUESTION 9

Some new drill bits cost $16.90 as the regular retail price. The store then has a 20% sale. How much will the drill bits cost during the sale?

Answer:

_____

QUESTION 10

If a 1200 amp jump-starter retails for $99, how much will it cost after the store takes off 30%?

Answer:

_____

Unit 9: Measurement Conversions

Short-answer questions

Specific instructions to students

- This unit is designed to help you both to improve your skills and to increase your speed in converting one measurement unit into another.
- Read the following questions and answer all of them in the spaces provided.
- No calculators.
- You will need to show all working.

QUESTION 1

How many millimetres are there in 1 cm?

Answer:

QUESTION 2

How many millimetres are there in 1 m?

Answer:

QUESTION 3

How many centimetres are there in 1 m?

Answer:

QUESTION 4

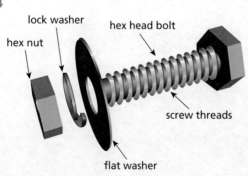

lock washer

hex head bolt

hex nut

screw threads

flat washer

If a screw has 20 threads in 2 cm, how many threads would there be in 10 cm?

Answer:

QUESTION 5

How many millilitres are there in 4.8 L of de-greaser?

Answer:

QUESTION 6

How many litres are there in 3500 mL of drain cleaner?

Answer:

QUESTION 7

A plumber's work van weighs ½ a tonne. How many kilograms is that?

Answer:

QUESTION 8

A workman's ute weighs 2 t. How many kilograms is that?

Answer:

QUESTION 9

A small truck carrying piping weighs 4750 kg. How many tonnes does it weigh?

Answer:

QUESTION 10

A trailer measures 180 cm in length and 120 cm across the back. How far is it around the perimeter of the trailer?

Answer:

9780170473378

Unit 10: Measurement – Length, Area and Volume

Section A: Circumference

Short-answer questions

Specific instructions to students

- This section is designed to help you both to improve your skills and to increase your speed in measuring the circumference of a round object.
- Read the following questions and answer all of them in the spaces provided.
- No calculators.
- You will need to show all working.

$C = \pi \times d$

where: C = circumference, π = 3.14 and d = diameter

EXAMPLE

Find the circumference of a pipe with a diameter of 30 cm.

$C = \pi \times d$

Therefore, $C = 3.14 \times 30$
$\qquad = 94.2$ cm

QUESTION 1

What is the circumference of a pulley with a diameter of 90 cm?

Answer:

QUESTION 2

Find the circumference of a mains pipe with a diameter of 15 cm.

Answer:

QUESTION 3

Calculate the circumference of a drainage pipe with a diameter of 32 cm.

Answer:

QUESTION 4

What is the circumference of a hose with a diameter of 5 cm?

Answer:

QUESTION 5

Find the circumference of machine hose with a diameter of 12 cm.

Answer:

QUESTION 6

Calculate the circumference of an industrial pipe with a diameter of 28.8 cm.

Answer:

QUESTION 7

What is the circumference of a can of grease with a diameter of 15.6 cm?

Answer:

QUESTION 8

Find the circumference of an angle grinder disc with a diameter of 14.3 cm.

Answer:

_____

QUESTION 9

Calculate the circumference of a toilet with a diameter of 42.9 cm.

Answer:

_____

QUESTION 10

Find the circumference of a sink with a diameter of 18.8 cm.

Answer:

_____

Section B: Diameter

Short-answer questions

Specific instructions to students

- This section is designed to help you both to improve your skills and to increase your speed in measuring the diameter of a round object.
- Read the following questions and answer all of them in the spaces provided.
- No calculators.
- You will need to show all working.

Diameter (D) of a circle $= \dfrac{\text{circumference}}{\pi(3.14)}$

EXAMPLE

Find the diameter of a sewer pipe with a circumference of 80 cm.

$D = \dfrac{80}{3.14} = 25.47$ cm

QUESTION 1

What is the diameter of a sink with a circumference of 120 cm?

Answer:

_____

QUESTION 2

Find the diameter of a flange with a circumference of 16 cm.

Answer:

_____

QUESTION 3

Calculate the diameter of a pipe with a circumference of 20 cm.

Answer:

_____

QUESTION 4

What is the diameter of a flange with a circumference of 100 cm?

Answer:

_____

QUESTION 5

Find the diameter of a rainwater tank with a circumference of 430 cm.

Answer:

_____

9780170473378

QUESTION 6

What is the diameter of a lock nut with a circumference 11.8 cm?

Answer:

_____

QUESTION 7

Find the diameter of a machine hose with a circumference of 12.4 cm.

Answer:

_____

QUESTION 8

Calculate the diameter of a sewer pipe with a circumference of 90.8 cm.

Answer:

_____

QUESTION 9

What is the diameter of a round toilet bowl with a circumference of 102.3 cm?

Answer:

_____

QUESTION 10

Find the diameter of an electric hot-water heater with a circumference of 260.8 cm.

Answer:

_____

Section C: Area

Area = length × breadth and is given in square units
= $l \times b$

QUESTION 1

A plumber's trailer is 1.8 m by 1.2 m wide. What is the total floor area?

Answer:

_____

QUESTION 2

A plumbing workshop's floor area measures 60 m by 13 m. What is the total area?

Answer:

_____

QUESTION 3

If a sheet of gyprock is 2.85 m by 1.65 m, what is the total area?

Answer:

_____

QUESTION 4

A welding space is 4.5 m × 1.8 m. What is the total area?

Answer:

_____

QUESTION 5

A roll of plastic sheet can be purchased by the square metre. What is the total area of a 30 m roll that is 1.50 m wide?

Answer:

_____

QUESTION 6

If a shower wall that needs sealing measures 1.95 m × 0.98 m, what is the total area of one wall?

Answer:

_____

QUESTION 7

The floor of the boot of a plumber's station wagon measures 1.06 m by 1.07 m. What is the total boot floor area?

Answer:

_____

QUESTION 8

An industrial plumbing storage area is 65.3 m × 32.7 m. How much floor area is there in total?

Answer:

_____

QUESTION 9

The dimensions of a floor area of a plumbing display at a hardware store measures 3.2 m wide by 8.6 m long. What is the total floor area?

Answer:

_____

QUESTION 10

A tray of a plumbing truck has a side that is 8.9 m long and is 2.6 m wide. How much floor area can it accommodate?

Answer:

_____

Section D: Volume of a cube

Short-answer questions

Specific instructions to students

- This section is designed to help you both to improve your skills and to increase your speed in calculating volume of rectangular or square objects.
- Read the following questions and answer all of them in the spaces provided.
- No calculators.
- You will need to show all working.

Volume = length × width × height and is given in cubic units

= $l \times w \times h$

QUESTION 1

How many cubic metres are there in a storage area measuring 13 m by 5 m by 4 m?

Answer:

QUESTION 2

A truck has the following dimensions: 8 m × 2 m × 3 m. How many cubic metres are available in the truck?

Answer:

QUESTION 3

If a semitrailer used for transporting plumbing accessories is 18 m long by 3 m high by 3 m wide, how much volume can it hold?

Answer:

QUESTION 4

A welder constructs a small trailer for a plumber to store his tools in, measuring 2.2 m × 1.8 m × 0.5 m. How much volume can it hold?

Answer:

QUESTION 5

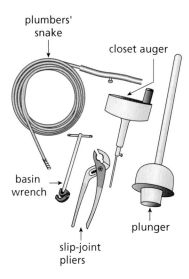

plumbers' snake

closet auger

basin wrench

plunger

slip-joint pliers

A trade assistant makes a new toolbox with the following dimensions: 0.6 m by 0.3 m by 0.15 m. How many cubic metres can the toolbox hold?

Answer:

QUESTION 6

A bathroom measures 1.5 m × 2.3 m × 2.1 m. What is its volume?

Answer:

QUESTION 7

A spare parts box is 1 m long, 0.6 m wide and 0.75 m tall. How much volume is available for storing parts?

Answer:

QUESTION 8

The boot of a station wagon is 1.4 m wide × 1.6 m long × 0.9 cm high. What is its volume in cubic metres?

Answer:

_____

QUESTION 9

A plumber buys a new van that is 1.75 m high by 1.35 m wide by 3.6 m long. What is its volume in cubic metres?

Answer:

_____

QUESTION 10

An apprentice needs to de-grease a workshop's walls and floor that measure 3.8 m by 3.8 m by 2.5 m. How many cubic metres need to be cleaned?

Answer:

_____

Section E: Volume of a cylinder

Short-answer questions

Specific instructions to students

- This section is designed to help you both to improve your skills and to increase your speed in calculating volume of cylinder-shaped objects.
- Read the following questions and answer all of them in the spaces provided.
- No calculators.
- You will need to show all working.

Volume of a cylinder $(V_c) = \pi$ **(3.14)** $\times r^2$ **(radius × radius) × height**

$V_c = \pi \times r^2 \times h$

QUESTION 1

What is the volume of a drum that is filled with cleaning fluid and that has a radius of 0.4 m and a height of 1.4 m?

Answer:

_____

QUESTION 2

What is the volume of a cylinder of joint sealant that has a radius of 3 cm and a height of 20 cm?

Answer:

_____

QUESTION 3

A hot-water tank has a radius of 1.2 m and a height of 2 m. What is its volume?

Answer:

_____

QUESTION 4

A grease gun has a radius of 3 cm and a length of 30 cm. How much grease can it hold?

Answer:

_____

QUESTION 5

A can of lubricant has a radius of 4 cm and a height of 20 cm. What is its volume?

Answer:

_____

9780170473378

QUESTION 6

A plumber's bottle of methylated spirits has a radius of 5 cm and a height of 25 cm.

a If the bottle was originally filled from a 4 L container, how much methylated spirits has been used?

Answer:

_____

b How much is left in the 4 L container?

Answer:

_____

QUESTION 7

A 5 L container of drain cleaner gets poured into 3 containers. Each container has a radius of 5 cm and a height of 20 cm.

a What is the volume of each container?

Answer:

_____

b What is the volume of all 3 containers in total?

Answer:

_____

c How much is left in the 5 L container?

Answer:

_____

QUESTION 8

A container of grease has a radius of 10 cm and a height of 15 cm.

a What is its volume?

Answer:

_____

b If you use half on one job, how much is left?

Answer:

_____

QUESTION 9

A container of general purpose thinners has a radius of 10 cm and a height of 20 cm.

a What is its volume?

Answer:

_____

b If you use 1750 mL, how much is left?

Answer:

_____

QUESTION 10

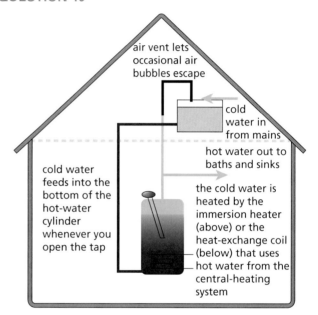

A plumber installs a hot-water unit that has a radius of 1.2 m and is 3.6 m high. What is its volume in cubic metres?

Answer:

_____

Unit 11: Earning Wages

Short-answer questions

Specific instructions to students

- This unit will help you to calculate both how much a job is worth and how long you need to complete the job.
- Read the following questions and answer all of them in the spaces provided.
- No calculators.
- You will need to show all working.

QUESTION 1

If a first-year plumbing apprentice earns $260.80 gross per week, how much does he earn per year?

Answer:

QUESTION 2

A plumber starts work at 8.00 a.m. and stops for a break at 10.30 a.m. He begins to work again at 10.50 a.m. and finishes at 12.50 p.m. for lunch. He then resumes work at 2.00 p.m. and continues until 4.00 p.m. How many hours and minutes has he worked, excluding the breaks?

Answer:

QUESTION 3

A trade assistant earns $15.50 an hour and works a 38-hour week. How much will her gross earnings be (before tax)?

Answer:

QUESTION 4

Over a week, a plumber completes 5 jobs that amount to the following: $465.80, $2490.50, $556.20, $1560.70 and $990.60. What does the total bill come to?

Answer:

QUESTION 5

A plumber needs to remove the following: piping (that takes 34 minutes); a tap (that takes 8 minutes); two tiles (that takes 7 minutes); the tiles around the vanity (that takes 24 minutes) and a door (that takes 9 minutes). How much time has been taken up in total on this job? State your answer in hours and minutes.

Answer:

QUESTION 6

A 6 m length of copper pipe needs to be removed before being replaced. This takes the plumber 4½ hours. If the rate of pay for labour is $28.60 per hour, how much will the plumber be paid for the time that he has worked?

Answer:

QUESTION 7

A small plumbing job takes 1½ hours to complete. If the plumber is getting paid $34.80 per hour, what is the total that she will earn?

Answer:

9780170473378

QUESTION 8

A leak in a bathroom causes major damage. The bath tiles, floor tiles and shower tiles need to be removed before the plumber and his apprentice can begin the plumbing work. They spend 104 hours in total working on this job. If they work 8 hours per day, how many days will it take?

Answer:

QUESTION 9

A plumber begins work at 8.00 a.m. and works until 4.00 p.m. She spends 20 minutes on her morning break, 60 minutes on her lunch break and 20 minutes on her afternoon break.

a   How much time has been spent on breaks in total?

Answer:

b   How much time has she spent working?

Answer:

QUESTION 10

A job costs $550.50 to complete. The plumber spends 12 hours on the job. How much is his hourly rate?

Answer:

Unit 12: Squaring Numbers

Section A: Introducing square numbers

Short-answer questions

Specific instructions to students

- This section is designed to help you both to improve your skills and to increase your speed in squaring numbers.
- Read the following questions and answer all of them in the spaces provided.
- No calculators.
- You will need to show all working.

Any number squared is multiplied by itself.

EXAMPLE

4 squared $= 4^2 = 4 \times 4 = 16$

QUESTION 1

$6^2 =$

Answer:

QUESTION 2

$8^2 =$

Answer:

QUESTION 3

$12^2 =$

Answer:

QUESTION 4

$3^2 =$

Answer:

QUESTION 5

$7^2 =$

Answer:

QUESTION 6

$11^2 =$

Answer:

QUESTION 7

$10^2 =$

Answer:

QUESTION 8

$9^2 =$

Answer:

QUESTION 9

$2^2 =$

Answer:

$4^2 =$

Answer:

$5^2 =$

Answer:

Section B: Applying square numbers to the trade

Worded practical problems

Specific instructions to students

- This section is designed to help you both to improve your skills and to increase your speed in calculating the area of rectangular or square objects. The worded questions make the content relevant to everyday situations.
- Read the following questions and answer all of them in the spaces provided.
- No calculators.
- You will need to show all working.

QUESTION 1

A plumber measures an area that will be used for a water tank. The area measures 2.8 m × 2.8 m. What area does it take up?

Answer:

QUESTION 2

A plumber's workshop has a work area that is 5.2 m × 5.2 m. What is the total area?

Answer:

QUESTION 3

The dimensions of a factory room that is to be plumbed are 12.6 m × 12.6 m. What is the total area?

Answer:

QUESTION 4

A plumbing accessories floor space measures 15 m^2. If there is an area allocated for the reception that is 2.4 m^2, how much floor space is left?

Answer:

QUESTION 5

A plumbing warehouse has an area set aside for equipment that measures 13.8 m^2. If the spare parts area takes up 1.2 m^2 and the tool area is 2.7 m^2, how much area is left?

Answer:

QUESTION 6

A plumber needs to remove a sheet from a wall that is 2.4 m². If he cuts out 1.65 m² to fit a vanity unit, how much sheet area is left?

Answer:

_____

QUESTION 7

A plumber cuts out a piece of 5 cm × 5 cm gyprock from a sheet that is 1.2 m². How much sheet area is left?

Answer:

_____

QUESTION 8

A concrete work floor measures 28 m × 28 m. If it costs $9.50 to seal 1 m², how much will it cost to seal the whole floor?

Answer:

_____

QUESTION 9

Each of the four walls of a workshop measures 2.6 m. To insulate 1 m², it costs $28.50. How much will it cost to insulate all four walls?

Answer:

_____

_____

_____

_____

QUESTION 10

Four walls of a workshop need to be painted. The total wall area measures 22 m². If it costs $6.80 to paint 1 m², how much will it cost to paint the 22 m²?

Answer:

_____

Section A: Introducing ratios

QUESTION 1

The number of teeth on gear cog 1 is 40. The number of teeth on gear cog 2 is 20. What is the ratio of gear cog 1 to gear cog 2?

Answer:

_____

QUESTION 2

Pulley A has a diameter of 60 cm and pulley B has a diameter of 15 cm. What is the ratio of diameter A to B?

Answer:

_____

QUESTION 3

Pulley belt A has a diameter of 48 cm and pulley belt B has a diameter of 16 cm. What is the ratio of diameter A to B?

Answer:

_____

QUESTION 4

Two gear cogs have 75 and 15 teeth respectively. What is the ratio of the cogs?

Answer:

_____

QUESTION 5

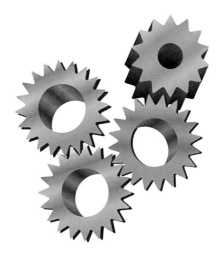

Three cogs have 80 : 60 : 20 teeth respectively. What is the ratio?

Answer:

_____

QUESTION 6

A lathe has 2 pulleys that have diameters of 16 cm and 20 cm respectively. What is the lowest ratio?

Answer:

_____

QUESTION 7

The diameter of pulley A on a band saw is 32 cm. Pulley B has a diameter of 16 cm and pulley C has a diameter of 48 cm. What is the lowest ratio of the three compared together?

Answer:

QUESTION 8

Three pulleys have different diameters: 18 cm, 16 cm and 10 cm respectively. What is the comparative ratio?

Answer:

QUESTION 9

Pulley A has a diameter of 34 cm and pulley B has a diameter of 12 cm. What is the ratio?

Answer:

QUESTION 10

The circumference of pulley A is 62 cm and the circumference of pulley B is 38 cm. What is the ratio?

Answer:

Section B: Applying ratios to the trade

Short-answer questions

Specific instructions to students

- This section is designed to help to improve your practical skills when working with ratios.
- Read the following questions and answer all of them in the spaces provided.
- No calculators.
- You will need to show all working.

QUESTION 1

The ratio of the teeth on cog 1 to cog 2 is 3 : 1. If cog 2 has 10 teeth, how many teeth will cog 1 have?

Answer:

QUESTION 2

The ratio of the teeth on cog 1 to cog 2 is 2 : 1. If cog 2 has 20 teeth, how many teeth will cog 1 have?

Answer:

QUESTION 3

The ratio of the diameter of pulley A to pulley B is 4 : 2. If pulley A has a diameter of 40 cm, what will be the diameter of pulley B?

Answer:

QUESTION 4

The ratio of the diameter of pulley A to pulley B is 2 : 1. If pulley A has a diameter of 30 cm, what will be the diameter of pulley B?

Answer:

The ratio of teeth on cog A to cog B is 3 : 1. If the number of teeth on cog A is 12, how many teeth are on cog B?

Answer:

_____

The ratio of teeth on cog A to cog B is 2 : 1. If the number of teeth on cog A is 18, how many teeth are on cog B?

Answer:

_____

The ratio of teeth on cog A to cog B is 3 : 1. If the number of teeth on cog A is 21, how many teeth are on cog B?

Answer:

_____

The ratio of teeth on cog A to cog B is 3 : 2. If the number of teeth on cog A is 6, how many teeth are on cog B?

Answer:

_____

The ratio of teeth on cog A to cog B is 4 : 3. If the number of teeth on cog A is 16, how many teeth will be on cog B?

Answer:

_____

The ratio of teeth on cog A to cog B is 4 : 3. If the number of teeth on cog A is 24, how many teeth will be on cog B?

Answer:

_____

Short-answer questions

Specific instructions to students

- This section is designed to help to improve your skills in calculating measurement and area using Pythagoras' theorem.
- Read the following questions and answer all of them in the spaces provided.
- You may use a calculator for this unit to check your answers.
- All working, including approximations, should be done by hand.

The following theorem applies to right-angled triangles, which are often encountered by workers in the plumbing industry.

$a^2 + b^2 = c^2$

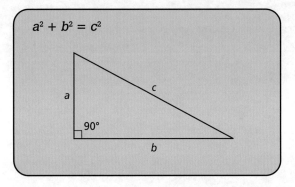

If we consider this formula as it applies to the plumbing trade, we can introduce the following terms.

a = side length 'a' (or run)

b = side length 'b' (or offset)

c = diagonal length

So if:

$a^2 + b^2 = c^2$

Then to solve for c (the diagonal length), you need to find the square root of $a^2 + b^2$.

To solve Questions 1–3, you will need to refer to the following example.

A plumber knows that side a is 2 m long and that side b is at a right angle to side a. He also knows that side b measures 3 m. He needs to fit a length of pipe to the diagonal side; however, he doesn't know the length of the diagonal. What is the length of the diagonal, c?

_____

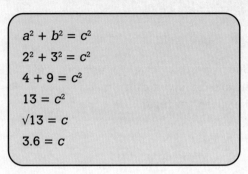

$$a^2 + b^2 = c^2$$
$$2^2 + 3^2 = c^2$$
$$4 + 9 = c^2$$
$$13 = c^2$$
$$\sqrt{13} = c$$
$$3.6 = c$$

Therefore, the pipe needs to measure 3.6 m for the diagonal length c.

QUESTION 1

If side a is 3 m and side b is 3 m, what is the length of the diagonal side c that needs to be cut?

Answer:

_____

QUESTION 2

If side a is 1 m and side b is 3 m, what is the length of the diagonal side c that needs to be cut?

Answer:

_____

QUESTION 3

If side a is 4 m and side b is 5 m, what is the length of the diagonal side c that needs to be cut?

Answer:

_____

Unit 15: Mechanical Reasoning

Short-answer questions

Specific instructions to students

- This section is designed to help to improve your skills in mechanical reasoning.
- Read the following questions and answer all of them in the spaces provided.
- No calculators.
- You will need to show all working.

QUESTION 1

If cog X turns in a clockwise direction, which way will cog Y turn?

Answer:

_____

QUESTION 2

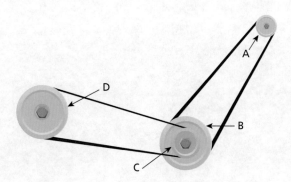

If pulley A turns in a clockwise direction, which way will pulley D turn?

Answer:

_____

QUESTION 3

If the drive pulley in the following diagram of a work van engine turns in a clockwise direction, in which direction will the alternator turn?

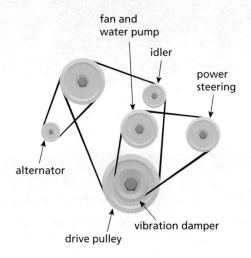

Answer:

_____

QUESTION 4

Looking at the following diagram, if lever A moves to the left, in which direction will lever B move?

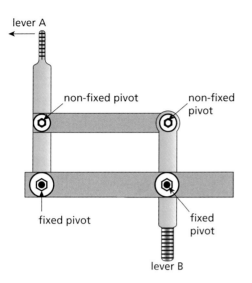

Answer:

_____

QUESTION 5

In the following diagram, pully 1 turns clockwise. In what direction will pully 6 turn?

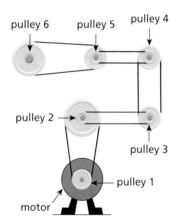

Answer:

_____

QUESTION 6

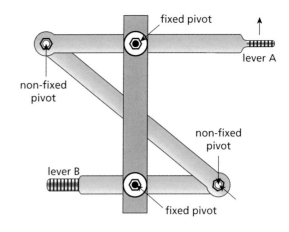

If lever A is pulled up, what will happen to lever B?

Answer:

_____

Plumbing
Practice Written Exam
for the Plumbing Trade

Reading time: 10 minutes

Writing time: 1 hour 30 minutes

Section A: Literacy

Section B: General Mathematics

Section C: Trade Mathematics

QUESTION and ANSWER BOOK

Section	Topic	Number of questions	Marks
A	Literacy	7	22
B	General Mathematics	11	26
C	Trade Mathematics	40	52
		Total 58	Total 100

The sections may be completed in the order of your choice.

NO CALCULATORS are to be used during the exam.

Spelling

Read the passage below and then underline the 20 spelling errors.

10 marks

Andrew the Plumber got an urgent phone call at 6.00 a.m. The house akross the road had sprung a leek. It was a two-story house and the toilat had started leaking upstairs. The residant did not notise the leak untill he had walked into the kitchan and saw a huge pudle of water on the floor. Gordy, who was Andrew's co-worker, was asked to atend as he had experiance in fixing upstairs toilets.

Within minates, both Andrew and Gordy were upstairs survaying the site of the leak. It was evidant that the water was coming out of the top of the cisstern. Gordy took the top off of the unit and peared inside. The float had come off and the water continued to flo after every flush. The resident had turned the water off at the maynes after he had scene the damage that had been caused downstairs. It took Gordy only a few minutes to reattach the float and to turn the water mains back on.

Correct the spelling errors by writing them out with the correct spelling below.

_____

_____

Alphabetising

Put the following words into alphabetical order.

7 marks

Ladder	Pipe wrench
Hacksaw	Laser level
Adjustable wrenches	Tape measure
Screwdrivers	Pipe fitters
Rib-joint pliers	Plunger
Locking pliers	Pipe benders
Pipe cutters	Drain unblocker

_____

_____

_____

_____

_____

_____

_____

_____

_____

_____

_____

_____

Comprehension

Short-answer questions

Specific instructions to students

- Read the passage and then answer the questions that follow.

On a cold winter morning, Dean received a call-out at 8.00 a.m. to a home owner out in the northern suburbs. She was having trouble with her toilet overflowing due to a problem with the sewerage pipe. Dean had been working for over 3 years as a plumber and he knew that this was a common problem. Next to the house, several large trees had established themselves and the roots of the trees had made their way into the sewerage pipe. Dean had to find out where the trees had been able to get into the sewerage pipe, which is a rich source of nutrients for the trees.

Dean traced the problem out to the front of the house where the main sewerage pipe was. He was able to find the cover for the pipe and he went back to his truck to get his rotor rooter (also called an electric eel). This was a long steel cable that could be rotated and twisted, and basically destroyed the root that had penetrated the sewerage pipe. It took around 70 minutes to mulch the roots as they were well established and had caused significant blockage. This blockage caused the water and sewage to back up in the pipes, and was the reason why the toilet was overflowing.

QUESTION 1	1 mark

At what time did Dean receive the call-out?

Answer:

_____

QUESTION 2	1 mark

What was the problem that Dean was called out to fix?

Answer:

_____

_____

_____

QUESTION 3   1 mark

What do trees and their roots find appealing about sewerage pipes?

Answer:

_____

_____

QUESTION 4   1 mark

What is a rotor rooter and what does it do?

Answer:

_____

_____

QUESTION 5   1 mark

What did the blockage cause throughout the house?

Answer:

_____

_____

Section B: General Mathematics

QUESTION 1   3 marks

What unit of measurement would you use to measure:

a   a length of pipe?

Answer:

_____

b   the temperature of water in a pipe?

Answer:

_____

c   the amount of pipe sealant?

_____

QUESTION 2   3 marks

Write an example of the following and give an instance where it may be found in the plumbing industry.

a   percentages

Answer:

_____

b   decimals

Answer:

_____

c   fractions

Answer:

_____

_____

QUESTION 3   2 marks

Convert the following units.

a   2 kg to grams

Answer:

_____

b   4000 g to kilograms.

Answer:

_____

QUESTION 4   2 marks

Write the following in descending order:

   0.7   0.71   7.1   70.1   701.00   7.0

Answer:

_____

QUESTION 5   2 marks

Write the decimal number that is between:

a 0.1 and 0.2

Answer:

_____

b 1.3 and 1.4

Answer:

_____

QUESTION 6   2 marks

Round off the following numbers to two (2) decimal places.

a 5.177

Answer:

_____

b 12.655

Answer:

_____

QUESTION 7   2 marks

Estimate the following by approximation.

a $101 \times 81 =$

Answer:

_____

b $399 \times 21 =$

Answer:

_____

QUESTION 8   2 marks

What do the following add up to?

a $7, $13.57 and $163.99

Answer:

_____

b 4, 5.73 and 229.57

Answer:

_____

QUESTION 9   2 marks

Subtract the following.

a 196 from 813

Answer:

_____

b 5556 from 9223

Answer:

_____

QUESTION 10   2 marks

Use division to solve:

a $4824 \div 3 =$

Answer:

_____

b $84.2 \div 0.4 =$

Answer:

_____

QUESTION 11   4 marks

Using BODMAS, solve:

a $(3 \times 7) \times 4 + 9 - 5 =$

Answer:

_____

b $(8 \times 12) \times 2 + 8 - 4 =$

Answer:

_____

Section C: Trade Mathematics

Basic operations

Addition

QUESTION 1   1 mark

An apprentice plumber uses 8 m, 6 m, 9 m and 4 m of conduit on a plumbing job. How much conduit has he used in total?

Answer:

_____

QUESTION 2   1 mark

A plumber charges $1075 for labour and $1983 for parts and accessories for a bathroom. How much is the total bill?

Answer:

_____

Subtraction

QUESTION 1   1 mark

A plumber fills his work van with 36 L of LPG. There was already some LPG in the tank, and combined with the 36 L, the tank is now at its maximum of 52 L. A driver uses the following amounts of LPG on each day:

Monday: 5 L

Tuesday: 11 L

Wednesday: 10 L

Thursday: 8 L

Friday: 7 L

How many litres of LPG are now left in the tank?

Answer:

_____

QUESTION 2   1 mark

If a plumber has 261 washers in stock and he uses 198 over 2 months, how many are left?

Answer:

_____

Multiplication

QUESTION 1   1 mark

A plumber uses 9 nuts, 18 washers and 9 bolts on a bathroom. How many nuts, washers and bolts would be used on 9 similar fixes?

Answer:

_____

QUESTION 2   1 mark

An apprentice plumber uses 2 m of 25 mm PVC pipe, 3 m of 50 mm PVC pipe and 1 m of 35 mm PVC pipe on a plumbing job. How much of each PVC pipe would be needed for 9 more similar jobs?

Answer:

_____

_____

Division

QUESTION 1   2 marks

An apprentice plumber has a box of 120 fasteners.

a How many jobs can the apprentice plumber complete if each standard job requires 8 fasteners?

Answer:

_____

b Will any fasteners be left over?

Answer:

_____

QUESTION 2   1 mark

If an apprentice earns $268.80 for working a 5-day week, how much does she earn per day?

Answer:

_____

Decimals

Addition

QUESTION 1   1 mark

A set of sockets and a pipe bender are purchased for $27.99 and $125.50 respectively. How much will be paid in total?

Answer:

QUESTION 2   1 mark

An apprentice plumber purchases a 7-piece flaring toolkit for $29.95, a Stillson pipe wrench for $24.95, a hole-saw kit for $55.95 and a sink/drain unblocking tool set for $39.50. How much has he spent in total?

Answer:

Subtraction

QUESTION 1   1 mark

A plumber has a 4 m length of 35 mm PVC to be used on three different jobs. He uses 1185 mm for job 1, 1560 mm for job 2 and 1135 mm for job 3. How much of the PVC is left?

Answer:

QUESTION 2   1 mark

A plumber has a 6 m length of conduit. If 2.78 m is used on one job, 1.76 m is used on a second job and 1.44 m is used on a third job, how much of the conduit is left on the reel?

Answer:

Multiplication

QUESTION 1   1 mark

A plumber replaces 6 drill bits at a cost of $6.99 each and then buys 4 quick-grip clamps at $5.99 each. What is the total amount that the plumber has spent?

Answer:

QUESTION 2   1 mark

If an apprentice plumber uses 6 packets of 50 mm screws that cost $9.50 per packet, how much is the total cost?

Answer:

Division

QUESTION 1   1 mark

A plumber takes 12 hours to complete 3 jobs. The total bill comes to $582.48. How much does the plumber charge per hour?

Answer:

QUESTION 2   1 mark

A plumbing company buys 240 pairs of safety glasses in bulk at a total cost of $2160. What is the cost of one pair?

Answer:

Fractions

QUESTION 1   1 mark

$\frac{2}{3} + \frac{3}{4} =$

Answer:

QUESTION 2   1 mark

$\frac{4}{5} - \frac{1}{3} =$

Answer:

QUESTION 3   1 mark

$\frac{2}{3} \times \frac{1}{4} =$

Answer:

QUESTION 4   1 mark

$$\frac{3}{4} \div \frac{1}{2} =$$

Answer:

___

Percentages

QUESTION 1   2 marks

A plumbing repair bill on a house comes to $1380.00.

a How much is 10% of the bill?

Answer:

___

b What is the final bill once 10% is taken off?

Answer:

___

QUESTION 2   2 marks

A plumber buys a tube pipe bender, a hammer and a new pair of multi-grip plumbing water pump pliers. The total comes to $170.50.

a How much is 10% of the bill?

Answer:

___

b What is the final total once 10% is taken off?

Answer:

___

Measurement conversions

QUESTION 1   1 mark

How many millimetres are there in 3.85 m?

Answer:

___

QUESTION 2   1 mark

Convert 2285 mm into metres.

Answer:

___

Measurement – length, area and volume

Circumference

QUESTION 1   1 mark

What is the circumference of a circular saw with a diameter of 24 cm?

Answer:

___

QUESTION 2   1 mark

What is the circumference of an orbital sander with a diameter of 15 cm?

Answer:

___

Diameter

QUESTION 1   1 mark

What is the diameter of a cut-off saw with a circumference of 115 cm?

Answer:

___

QUESTION 2   1 mark

What is the diameter of a disc on an angle grinder with a circumference of 32 cm?

Answer:

___

Area

QUESTION 1   1 mark

A plumber's workshop floor measures 20 m by 21.2 m. What is the total area?

Answer:

___

QUESTION 2　　　　　　　　　　1 mark

The floor of a bathroom measures 3.2 m long by 1.5 m wide. How much floor area is there?

Answer:

_____

Volume of a cube

QUESTION 1　　　　　　　　　　1 mark

A small trailer measures 2 m × 2 m × 0.5 m. How many cubic metres is that?

Answer:

_____

QUESTION 2　　　　　　　　　　1 mark

A new toolbox has the following dimensions: 60 cm × 15 cm × 10 cm. What is the total volume?

Answer:

_____

Volume of a cylinder

QUESTION 1　　　　　　　　　　1 mark

A tube of liquid nails has a radius of 3 cm and a length of 30 cm. What volume is the tube?

Answer:

_____

QUESTION 2　　　　　　　　　　2 marks

A container of pipe weld glue has a radius of 8 cm and a height of 12 cm.

a　What is its volume?

Answer:

_____

b　If you use half on one job, how much is left?

Answer:

_____

Earning wages

QUESTION 1　　　　　　　　　　1 mark

A first-year apprentice plumber earns $270.60 net (take home) per week. How much does she earn per year? (Note that there are 52 weeks in a year.)

Answer:

_____

QUESTION 2　　　　　　　　　　1 mark

A house has major water damage from a leak. The labour bill comes to $2860. If the plumber spends 48 hours working on the house, what is the rate for labour per hour?

Answer:

_____

Squaring numbers

QUESTION 1　　　　　　　　　　1 mark

What is 8^2?

Answer:

_____

QUESTION 2　　　　　　　　　　1 mark

A workshop has an area of 5.2 m by 2.2 m. What is the total area?

Answer:

_____

Ratios

QUESTION 1　　　　　　　　　　1 mark

A driver cog has 20 teeth and the driven cog has 60 teeth. What is the ratio, in the lowest form, of the driver cog to the driven cog?

Answer:

_____

QUESTION 2   1 mark

The ratio of the diameters of driver pulley A to driven pulley B is 1 : 4. If the diameter of driver pulley A is 15 cm, what is the diameter of driven pulley B?

Answer:

_____

Pythagoras' theorem

QUESTION 1   2 marks

Two pipes are laid at right angles to one another. They are joined with a right-angled elbow joint. If the lengths of each pipe are 2 m and 4 m respectively, what distance are the ends from each other? (Hint: Draw a diagram before you begin calculating.)

Answer:

_____

QUESTION 2   2 marks

Two pipes are laid at right angles to one another. They are joined with a right-angled elbow joint. If the lengths of each pipe are 3 m and 5 m respectively, what distance are the ends directly from each other? (Hint: Draw a diagram before you begin calculating.)

Answer:

_____

Mechanical reasoning

QUESTION 1   2 marks

Pully 1 and pully 2 each measure 5 cm across their diameters. Pully 3 measures 10 cm across the diameter. How many times will pulleys 1 and 2 turn if pully 3 turns 3 times?

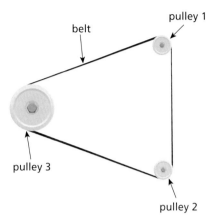

Answer:

_____

QUESTION 2   2 marks

Each cog in the following diagram has 16 teeth and they interlock with each other. If cog 5 turns in an anticlockwise direction, which way will cog 1 turn?

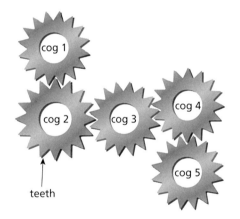

Answer:

_____

Glossary

Acrylic A thermoplastic that is heat activated and is used on surfaces, such as baths. It comes in sheets and has a fiberglass backing that helps to form waterproof shower walls

Ballcock The valve that controls the flow of water from the line of the water supply into a gravity-operated toilet tank. A float mechanism controls the tank water

Circumference The perimeter of a circle

Closet A term that can be used for a toilet

Diameter A line passing through the centre of a circle, extending from one side of the circumference to the other

Drop Vertical distance down

Effluent Septic system liquid waste

Elbow A pipe fitting with two openings that changes the direction of the line. It can come in a variety of angles, from 22.5° to 90°

Grade The difference in degrees between the run and drop. It can allow for water to run off into a drain or trap

O-ring A round rubber washer used to create a watertight seal, chiefly around valve stems

Perimeter The length of a boundary around a shape

Radius The shortest distance from the centre of a circle to the circumference

Run The horizontal distance usually along the ground and/or floor

Formulae and data

Circumference of a Circle

$C = \pi \times d$
where: C = circumference, π = 3.14, d = diameter

Diameter of a Circle

Diameter (d) of a circle = $\dfrac{\text{circumference}}{\pi(3.14)}$

Area

Area = length $\times$ breadth and is given in square units
$\quad$ = $l \times b$

Volume of a Cube

Volume = length $\times$ width $\times$ height and is given in cubic units
$\quad\quad$ = $l \times w \times h$

Volume of a Cylinder

Volume of a cylinder (V_c) = $\pi\,(3.14) \times r^2$ (r^2 = radius $\times$ radius) $\times$ height
$V_c = \pi \times r^2 \times h$

Pythagoras' Theorem

$a^2 + b^2 = c^2$

Times Tables

1

1 × 1	=	1
2 × 1	=	2
3 × 1	=	3
4 × 1	=	4
5 × 1	=	5
6 × 1	=	6
7 × 1	=	7
8 × 1	=	8
9 × 1	=	9
10 × 1	=	10
11 × 1	=	11
12 × 1	=	12

2

1 × 2	=	2
2 × 2	=	4
3 × 2	=	6
4 × 2	=	8
5 × 2	=	10
6 × 2	=	12
7 × 2	=	14
8 × 2	=	16
9 × 2	=	18
10 × 2	=	20
11 × 2	=	22
12 × 2	=	24

3

1 × 3	=	3
2 × 3	=	6
3 × 3	=	9
4 × 3	=	12
5 × 3	=	15
6 × 3	=	18
7 × 3	=	21
8 × 3	=	24
9 × 3	=	27
10 × 3	=	30
11 × 3	=	33
12 × 3	=	36

4

1 × 4	=	4
2 × 4	=	8
3 × 4	=	12
4 × 4	=	16
5 × 4	=	20
6 × 4	=	24
7 × 4	=	28
8 × 4	=	32
9 × 4	=	36
10 × 4	=	40
11 × 4	=	44
12 × 4	=	48

5

1 × 5	=	5
2 × 5	=	10
3 × 5	=	15
4 × 5	=	20
5 × 5	=	25
6 × 5	=	30
7 × 5	=	35
8 × 5	=	40
9 × 5	=	45
10 × 5	=	50
11 × 5	=	55
12 × 5	=	60

6

1 × 6	=	6
2 × 6	=	12
3 × 6	=	18
4 × 6	=	24
5 × 6	=	30
6 × 6	=	36
7 × 6	=	42
8 × 6	=	48
9 × 6	=	54
10 × 6	=	60
11 × 6	=	66
12 × 6	=	72

7

1 × 7	=	7
2 × 7	=	14
3 × 7	=	21
4 × 7	=	28
5 × 7	=	35
6 × 7	=	42
7 × 7	=	49
8 × 7	=	56
9 × 7	=	63
10 × 7	=	70
11 × 7	=	77
12 × 7	=	84

8

1 × 8	=	8
2 × 8	=	16
3 × 8	=	24
4 × 8	=	32
5 × 8	=	40
6 × 8	=	48
7 × 8	=	56
8 × 8	=	64
9 × 8	=	72
10 × 8	=	80
11 × 8	=	88
12 × 8	=	96

9

1 × 9	=	9
2 × 9	=	18
3 × 9	=	27
4 × 9	=	36
5 × 9	=	45
6 × 9	=	54
7 × 9	=	63
8 × 9	=	72
9 × 9	=	81
10 × 9	=	90
11 × 9	=	99
12 × 9	=	108

10

1 × 10	=	10
2 × 10	=	20
3 × 10	=	30
4 × 10	=	40
5 × 10	=	50
6 × 10	=	60
7 × 10	=	70
8 × 10	=	80
9 × 10	=	90
10 × 10	=	100
11 × 10	=	110
12 × 10	=	120

11

1 × 11	=	11
2 × 11	=	22
3 × 11	=	33
4 × 11	=	44
5 × 11	=	55
6 × 11	=	66
7 × 11	=	77
8 × 11	=	88
9 × 11	=	99
10 × 11	=	110
11 × 11	=	121
12 × 11	=	132

12

1 × 12	=	12
2 × 12	=	24
3 × 12	=	36
4 × 12	=	48
5 × 12	=	60
6 × 12	=	72
7 × 12	=	84
8 × 12	=	96
9 × 12	=	108
10 × 12	=	120
11 × 12	=	132
12 × 12	=	144

Multiplication Grid

	1	2	3	4	5	6	7	8	9	10	11	12
1	1	2	3	4	5	6	7	8	9	10	11	12
2	2	4	6	8	10	12	14	16	18	20	22	24
3	3	6	9	12	15	18	21	24	27	30	33	36
4	4	8	12	16	20	24	28	32	36	40	44	48
5	5	10	15	20	25	30	35	40	45	50	55	60
6	6	12	18	24	30	36	42	48	54	60	66	72
7	7	14	21	28	35	42	49	56	63	70	77	84
8	8	16	24	32	40	48	56	64	72	80	88	96
9	9	18	27	36	45	54	63	72	81	90	99	108
10	10	20	30	40	50	60	70	80	90	100	110	120
11	11	22	33	44	55	66	77	88	99	110	121	132
12	12	24	36	48	60	72	84	96	108	120	132	144

Notes

Notes

Notes

Notes

Notes

Notes

Notes